D1463247

Published by:
Joanne Frances Press
Oakland, Michigan

Imagine This! books may be purchased for educational, business, or sales promotional use.
For information, please contact:
Special Markets Division, Joanne Frances Press
PO Box 324 • Romeo, MI 48065 • 1-800-960-2347
www.JoanneFrancesPress.com

Printed and bound in Canada by Friesens of Altona, Manitoba

Digital Imaging by: Greg Dunn, Digital Imagery LLC
Type and graphic design by: Karen McDiarmid

Froh, Joanne
Imagine This! / written by Joanne Froh, illustrated by Frances Plagens
SUMMARY: A unique collection of original poems and illustrations for children
that will encourage them to use their own imaginations as they
celebrate the world of make-believe.

ISBN: 0-9777640-0-1

Library of Congress Control Number: 2006901533

Imagine This!

Poetry by Joanne Froh

Illustrations by Frances Plagens

J Joanne Frances Press

Dedicated to children everywhere who like to
daydream and play make-believe.
And for those of you who don't — well, this book is dedicated
to you also, in the hope that you will soon discover
what you've been missing ~ and join in the fun.

Imagination

Come, come and build a dream
things are not just what they seem.
Sing a song, tell a tale
Race along the magic trail.

Flying

WHAT a feeling it would be
　　to fly wherever I go,
And hear the startled cries
　　of all my friends below.

Little faces looking up
　　to watch me soar and glide
Waving, jumping, calling out
　　hoping for a ride.

To float above the houses
　　and look down upon the trees
Oh, I wish I could fly, don't you?
　　fly whenever I please.

The Warrior

A broken stick
And trash can lid
Became my sword and shield
As I faced the bear
Who swayed and snarled
And scratched the frosty air.

Breath like steam
Rose from his mouth
Black eyes locked onto mine
This is my dare
He seemed to say
Beware, young man, beware.

Soft and low
His growl began
Like thunder in his throat
Then I watched him rise
And stand on two
Which made him twice my size.

Then, from afar
My father's call
Reached me through the trees.
I had to leave
Though no great loss
'Twas only make-believe.

Daydream Horse

MY horse is wild but tame
Whenever I call his name
With flying mane, he comes to me
And paws the ground playfully.

He knows it's time
For me to climb
Upon his back and settle in
Like an open hand and resting chin
I sit alone
Upon my roan.

Pressing my knees to his sides
He understands and abides
First a walk, then galloping fast
To race the shadow we cast.

We run and run
Because it's fun
Like rolling waves across the sea
In perfect rhythm, my horse and me
Salt and pepper
Friends forever.

Gone Fishing

ONE day last summer
When I was seven
I went on a boat
With my Uncle Kevin.
We went fishing
On a small quiet lake
We left before dawn
I was barely awake.

We motored around
Then stopped at the spot
Where fish like to hide
When the weather is hot.
Casting our lines
With barely a ripple
We fished for an hour
With nary a nibble.

I stared at the water
And tried to see down
But my reflection
Was all that I found.
And that is when
I had a thought, a wish
That I could breathe water
And swim like a fish.

I'd go down deep
Where the water is cool
Where there isn't much light
And the big fish rule.
Then I could see
And know what they do
As we sit here on top
Staring into the blue.

Ha, ha, they say
We know you're there
We know your game
And we just don't care.
We're pretty darn smart
We'll sit here and wait
Sneak up from behind
Then steal your bait!

Secret Gate

COME with me on tiptoe feet
through my secret gate
There in silent soft retreat
a magic world does wait.

There beneath the shadowed vine
　　we'll play 'let's pretend'
And time will be like sunshine
　　that never seems to end.

With tiny twigs and green leaves
　　we'll make a pot of soup
And anyone who believes
　　can gladly have a scoop.

That's my mother's voice, I fear
　　calling me away —
Let's pretend we cannot hear
　　and linger just to play.

Pirate's Treasure

THE cave was dark and smelled of stale air,
From somewhere the sound of water dripping
...and cold.

My feet disturbed the thick gray dust
that had drifted down from rocks decaying
...and old.

I saw treasure heaped in chain-bound chests
Glinting in the dark — rubies, emeralds
...and gold.

Nearby, white bones lay scattered about
All that remained of pirates who'd quarreled
...and died.

In my dream, I ran from the cave
Taking a coin lest my friends would believe
...I lied.

Then, I awoke and lay on my bed
The vision of treasure still in my head
...and sighed.

Daytime
Dreams

I'D like to be an artist
And paint what isn't there
Glittering jewels like rainbow drops
Shimmering in the air.

On second thought, I see me
Climbing through the mist
To the top of jungle mountains
I'll be a scientist.

Or maybe I'd rather be
The one who can't be caught
Flying to the moon and back
I choose an astronaut!

Of course there are quiet things
A spy undercover
Stopping crime around the world
With secrets I discover.

Daytime dreams are so much fun
I do find them amusing.
To be what I want to be is just
A matter of choosing.

Rope Swing

IN the playground, at my school
There's a swing, and there's a rule
No standing in the seat
It's for your bottom, not your feet.
That's why I say
I'd rather play
On a rope, hung in a tree
So I can swing, wild and free
Swing like a chimpanzee.

With a rope, unlike chain
There's no one-way, no refrain
I can stand and swing tall
Or scrunch down and swing in a ball
Go left, right, twirl around
Faster, higher above the ground.

And if I run with all my might
I'm like a bird, taking flight
Defying gravity
Looking down on scenery
That's when it seems
That all my dreams
Can come — will come true
A preview
Of what's to be
It's all a possibility.

Pillow Pet

I have a leopard pillow cat
that sits upon my bed.
A special soft and furry place
to rest my tired head.

I wish that she could be alive
   to really talk and play.
We'd explore the jungle trails
   and while the hours away.

And when each day came to an end
   we'd curl side by side.
I'd go to sleep and she would stay
   alert and watchful-eyed.

The Dark

Tap, tap

What was that?
Straight up in bed I sat
Eyes wide open peering, listening
Listening for something nearing.
Something creeping down the hall?
Its shadow cast upon the wall?

In my room, late at night
When the house is still and there's no light
Things I know for sure are there
Clothes, toys and teddy bear
Seem to change
And rearrange
From stuff I love, to things I dread
From far away, to near the bed.
So I listen…

I hear my heart within my ears
Beating loud with all my fears.
And just when I think I'll run away
The black gets lighter, turns to gray.
Nothing happens, minutes pass
Like raindrops down a window glass.

I take a deep breath and realize
My imagination has tricked my eyes.
All that was, is still is
So off I go, to sleep that is.

Tissued Wings

I dream of a sylvan fairy glade
  where only I can go
Flickering with golden dappled shade
  and dew wet grass aglow.

I dream of the silver radiance
   of tiny tissued wings
On fairies doing their mystic dance
   around the toadstool rings.

And if I find they're but dragonflies
   darting from weed to weed
Should I believe only in my eyes
   or go where dreams can lead?

Always Remember…

A box is not a box
If you can climb inside
Put the door on the floor
Cut a window in the side.

A castle? A cave?
A great place to hide?
Whatever it is
It's yours to decide.

Do you have a favorite poem?

Each illustrated poem in the Imagine This!
collection is available as wall art.
To purchase enlargements, please visit:

www.JoanneFrances.com